THE GAME IN REVERSE

THE GAME

POEMS BY

IN REVERSE

TASLIMA NASRIN

Translated from the Bengali by

CAROLYNE WRIGHT

with Farida Sarkar, Mohammad Nurul Huda,

and Subharanjan Dasgupta

George Braziller   *New York*

Published in the United States by George Braziller, Inc., 1995

For information, please write to the publisher:

George Braziller, Inc.
60 Madison Avenue
New York, NY 10010

Grateful acknowledgment is made to the editors of the following publications in which, to the best of our knowledge, the below-listed poems appeared for the first time in English translation: *Grand Street* ("Body Theory," "Another Life"), *Index on Censorship* ("Border"), *Indiana Review* ("The Game in Reverse"), *London Review of Books* ("Border," "Divorce Letter"), *The New Yorker* ("At the Back of Progress . . . ," "Character," "Happy Marriage," "Things Cheaply Had"), *PEN American Center Newsletter* ("Character"), *Triquarterly* ("Happy Marriage," "Things Cheaply Had").

Library of Congress Cataloging-in-Publication Data:

Nasarina, Tasalima
    The game in reverse: poems/by Tasllima Nasrin ;
translated from the Bengali by Carolyne Wright
        p.   cm.
ISBN 0–8076–1392–4 (pbk.)
1. Bengali poetry—Translation into English.
2. Women—Bangladesh—Poetry. 3. Women—
Bangladesh—Crimes Against—Poetry. I Title.
PK1771.E3N37   1995   95-1780
891'.4417—dc20   CIP

Designed by Vincent Torre

Printed and bound in the United States

Table of Contents

I

from *Amar kichu jay ase na*
(*I Couldn't Care Less*), 1988 and 1990

I I

from *Nirbasita bahire antare*
(*Banished Without and Within*), 1989 and 1990

I I I

from *Atale antarin*

(*Captive in the Abyss*), 1991

IV

from *Behula eka bhasiyechila bhela*
(*Behula Floated the Raft Alone*), 1993;
and *Ay kasta jhepe, jiban debo mepe*
(*Pain Come Pouring Down, I'll Measure Out My Life for You*), 1994

Acknowledgments

The translator wishes to thank the Mary Ingraham Bunting Institute of Radcliffe College, the Fulbright Fellowship Program (through the Council for International Exchange of Scholars), the Department of Sanskrit and Indian Studies of Harvard University, the Smithsonian Institution, the United States Information Agency, and the Witter Bynner Foundation for Poetry for grants, fellowships, and research affiliations that made possible the undertaking and completion of this translation project.

Special thanks are also due to Mohammad Nurul Huda and Farida Sarkar, with whom I worked to prepare initial English versions and finalize completed translations of about half the poems; to Parameswari Ray Choudhury and Nandana Dev Sen, with whom I went over final versions of all poems completed; and to Taslima Nasrin herself.

Carolyne Wright

Poems in this collection appeared originally in Bengali in the following volumes:

Bamladesher nirbacita kabita (*Selected Poetry of Bangladesh*), edited by
Mohammad Nurul Huda. Dhaka: Muktadhara, 1988.

Amar kichu jay ase na (*I Couldn't Care Less*).
Mymensingh: Sakal, 1988. Republished in Dhaka by Vidyaprakas, 1990.

Nirbasita bahire antare (*Banished Without and Within*).
Mymensingh: Sakal, 1989. Republished in Dhaka by Vidyaprakas, 1990.

Atale antarin (*Captive in the Abyss*). Dhaka: Vidyaprakas, 1991.

Behula eka bhasiyechila bhela (*Behula Floated the Raft Alone*).
Dhaka: Sikha Prakasani, 1993.

Ay kasta jhepe, jiban debo mepe (*Pain Come Pouring Down, I'll Measure Out My Life
for You*). Jnankos Prakasani, 1994.

Preface

Taslima Nasrin was born in 1962 in Mymensingh, Bangladesh, daughter of a medical doctor and a housewife, both devoutly observant Muslims. She is third of four children, with two older brothers and a younger sister. Although she loved painting and had a youthful interest in architecture, she ultimately followed in her father's career, studying at the Mymensingh Medical College and receiving a M.B.B.S. (Bachelor of Medicine and Bachelor of Surgery) in 1984. With this degree, she completed her residency in the capital, Dhaka, and was later posted as a physician and government medical officer in Dhaka hospitals, among them the Sir Sallimullah Medical College and Mitford Hospital, where she served as a gynecologist and anesthesiologist.

Despite her medical training and career, Taslima Nasrin first became well known in Bangladesh in the late 1980s as a poet, columnist, novelist, and fiercely independent feminist, renowned for her bold criticisms of Bengali society. In 1989, Nasrin began to write columns for various newspapers and magazines. Through these columns as well as the publication of her poetry, Nasrin gradually became a household name among Bangladeshi intellectuals, gaining many admirers as well as critics.

In 1990, Nasrin faced her first public ordeal when columns she had written that were critical of Muslim religious scriptures led to outraged protests and demonstrations in Dhaka by militant Muslim groups, who demanded her public trial and execution. Despite these threats, Nasrin completed several short volumes over the next two years and received several awards, including Calcutta's prestigious Ananda Prize. But her precarious situation did not alter, and in January 1993, the Bangladesh authorities confiscated her passport.

One month later, in February 1993, Nasrin published a short novel, *Lajja* (*Shame*, after Salman Rushdie's book of the same title). The book was based in part on news reports of violence following the destruction of the Babri Masjid mosque, in India, by Hindu extremists. The novel depicted a fictional Bangladeshi Hindu family that suffers atrocities at the hands of Muslim fundamentalists in retribution for the attack on the mosque. Muslim fundamentalists then accused Nasrin of conspiracy against Islam and placed advertisements in major newspapers offering a reward of 50,000 *taka* ($1250) to anyone who would take her life. After the bounty was first advertised, Nasrin petitioned the Bangladeshi government for protection and the return of her passport, and eventually two police guards were posted around the clock at her apartment door. Months of international diplomatic and human-rights efforts partially succeeded when the Bangladeshi government returned Nasrin's passport in late April of 1994.

In early May 1994, Nasrin was in Calcutta, where she gave an interview to a reporter for the English-language daily, *The Statesman.* The interview, which was conducted in Bengali, quoted her as saying that "the Koran should be revised thoroughly." Nasrin immediately protested that she had been misquoted, and sent a letter of clarification to *The Statesman.* The letter stated, essentially, that she advocated changes not to the Koran but to the Sharia, the texts of Islamic law, to give equal status to men and women. She argued that the Koran and other religious texts were outdated, so "the question of revision is irrelevant."

The next month, the interview and Nasrin's letter were printed in a newspaper in Bangladesh, but her attempts at explanation only exacerbated the fury of conservatives. Fundamentalists felt that asserting the obsolescence of the Koran in the modern world was even worse than calling for its revision. In Bangladesh, Muslim militants staged massive demonstrations throughout the capital, demanding Nasrin's execution for blasphemy. Another radical Muslim cleric doubled the previous bounty offer to 100,000 *taka* ($2,500). Under intense pressure from fundamentalists, the Bangladeshi government issued a no-bail warrant for Nasrin's arrest. Their charge against Nasrin of blasphemy was based on an obscure, British-era statute outlawing acts that could offend religious sentiments—a law originally enacted, ironically enough, to diffuse tensions among religious communities.

At this point, Nasrin went into hiding. In August, 1994, after appearing before the High Court of Bangladesh, she was permitted to accept an offer of asylum from Sweden, where she arrived as a guest of the Swedish PEN writers' organization. While fundamentalist demands for Nasrin's extradition to Bangladesh have continued, she remains in Sweden, where she continues to write and publish. In November 1994, Nasrin traveled to Prague for the International PEN Congress, where the European Parliament announced that she had won the Sakharov Prize for Freedom of Thought.

Carolyne Wright

Translator's Note

In this collection, I have tried to provide a generous representative selection of Taslima Nasrin's poetry from this first decade of her book publishing career. The first three sections contain translations of the nineteen poems that I completed in Bangladesh in 1990 and 1991 with collaborators Farida Sarkar and Mohammad Nurul Huda. These poems were from *Amar kichu jay ase na* (*I Couldn't Care Less*), *Nirbasita bahire antare* (*Banished Without and Within*), and *Atale antarin* (*Captive in the Abyss*), Nasrin's first three full-length books.

For these poems, a preliminary English version was produced that conveyed accurately the sense of the original Bengali, even if the phrasing was awkward in English. The next phase was to sit down with the co-translator and go through the Bengali poem word for word. We noted the literal word order, idiomatic phrases, word play, and level of diction—the formality or familiarity of verb conjugations, pronouns, nouns, and adjectives, whether they were standard or colloquial Bengali (analogous in English to common words of Anglo-Saxon origin) or "high" Sanskritic derivation (analogous in English to words of Latin or Greek origin). My native-speaking collaborators alerted me to cultural information built into the poems' language through proverbial expressions, allusions to Indian and Bangladeshi history or mythology, and references to customs and traditions with which the poet would expect Bengali readers to be familiar.

The next step in the translation process was to combine elements from the collaborators' draft with the word-for-word literal version and the relevant cultural information, to create a final English translation that was as faithful as possible to the original in meaning and tone, and also successful as a poem in its own right. Having immersed myself as best I could in the life of the original poem, I tried to render its translation as if Taslima Nasrin had been writing in English.

Nasrin was present at many of the group sessions with Mohammad Nurul Huda and me. She listened while Huda and I went over my versions; if there were questions about her meaning, she explained in Bengali.

After I returned to the United States, when Nasrin's case began to make international headlines, journalists, editors, and human rights activists contacted me, very interested in her writing. It became clear that a book-length collection of Nasrin's poetry in English translation would be necessary. In 1993 and 1994, I translated a number of other poems from her first three books, checking these carefully with Parameswari Ray Choudhury and Nandana Dev Sen, Bengali colleagues based in the Boston area. For a few of these translations, Farida Sarkar also provided some suggestions by mail. Nasrin then indicated that she would like to incorporate some poems from two of her more recent books in the final section of this volume. Consulting English versions by Subharanjan Dasgupta that Nasrin provided, I completed translations of eleven poems from these two books and reviewed these with Nandana Dev Sen.

In these translations, I have endeavored to let Taslima Nasrin speak for herself, without interpretations, glosses, or undue embellishment. Notes occur where there is cultural information built into the poem's language through proverbial expressions, and where Nasrin makes allusions to Bangladeshi history, Muslim or Hindu lore, and references to customs and traditions that would be familiar to Bengali readers. Such information will, I hope, help English-language readers appreciate the rich, vibrant, and sometimes turbulent cultural milieu out of which these poems emerge and to gain an understanding of the conflicts and concerns that have catapulted Nasrin to global prominence.

Carolyne Wright

I

FROM

Amar kichu jay ase na
(I Couldn't Care Less)

1988 and 1990

Believing Hands

I'm neither on the right nor on the left.
    I am on my soil.

It's not religion, but the disciplined crowds
    of working people I want;
not murder, but the pure, graceful faces
    of people who seek truth.

I want the ways of art worthy of my soil.
I want the politics worthy of my soil.
I'm neither on the right nor on the left.
    I am on my soil.
It's not armaments, but garments I want
    on people's naked bodies;
not hunger, but nectar I want
    for people's withered hearts;
not drums, but crumbs I want
    in scarcity's drab cottages.
I want a house worth living in on my soil
    and the certainty of living until death.
It's not begging, but learning I want
    for oppressed, orphaned lives;
not a needy, but a healthy child I want
    in every tortured home.

Pouring the oppressors' blood out on my soil
        I shall push gloom aside,
so I've opened my hands wide
    under the abundant sun.
I want thousands upon thousands of believing hands
in these hands of mine.

Character

You're a girl
and you'd better not forget
that when you cross the threshold of your house
men will look askance at you.
When you keep on walking down the lane
men will follow you and whistle.
When you cross the lane and step onto the main road
men will revile you and call you a loose woman.

If you've got no character
you'll turn back,
and if you have
you'll keep on going,
     as you're going now.

Run! Run!

A pack of dogs is after you.
Remember, rabies.

A pack of men is after you.
Remember, syphilis.

Divided

He is your father, really he's no one to you.
He is your brother, really he's no one to you.
She is your sister, really she's no one to you.
She is your mother, really she's no one to you.
You are alone.
Those who call you friend, they too are no one to you.
You are alone.

When you weep, your finger
wipes the tears from your eyes, that finger is your own.
When you walk, your feet
when you speak, your tongue
when you laugh, your cheerful eyes are your friends.

Except for yourself you have no one,
no animal or plant.

But as much as you say you are yours,
are you really?

Tongue

Now people don't praise other people anymore.
They tame dogs in the house, two or three gray cats.
People now bathe and feed their dogs,
they heap lavish praise
on the manners and conduct, the names and fame of their cats.

People now gossip loudly
about thread, wood, and coal.
But so what
if the tongue's nature changes,
even though it praises bricks, wood, and stones.

Simple Talk

As it roamed around, a chromosome named X
fastened itself to another chromosome named X;
it could have fastened itself to another chromosome named Y.
There's no fundamental difference between X and Y,
just as there is none between A and B, or between R
and S. Neither A nor B is less than the other,
the weight or volume of O or P is not less than
the other's, just as between X and Y
      one is not less valuable
than the other.

From XX a person is born, from XY also
a person is born. Except for a few physical traits
there are no differences between them. They laugh, cry, eat,
sleep. Little by little they grow up
      with their human faults and virtues.
Neither is less significant than the other.

There's no reason for them to be divided, yet one group
promptly grabbed for its portion the cushioned chair,
the thick mattress on the bed, eighty percent of the property
      and the head of the fish.
On another plate lay the leftovers and the bones,
lay the bottles of cheap *alta* and scented hair oil.

Between X and Y, there is no relationship of eighty
and twenty, high and low, more and less. Yet
Y sits, mounted on the shoulders of X; Y is cheerfully
swinging its legs, whistling and flapping
      its arms. At the nape

of X's neck there's an ulcer, there are pains
     in X's knee, and cramps at the waist.
We all see these disparities before our eyes. But none of us
utters a word. Our tongues are cut, our lips stitched, our
hands are tied, our feet in shackles.

Shall none of us ever say a word?

Boundary

After she was enlightened and therefore wished to see
    the world's shapes and scents and colors,
she wanted to step out over the threshold;
they told her——*No.* This wall is the horizon line,
this roof terrace is your sky.
This bed and bolster, scented soap, talcum powder,
this onion and garlic, this needle and thread,
    lazy afternoons embroidering red and blue flowers
on the pillowcases, this portion is your life.

When she opened the main gate's black padlock
to see how much land there was to wander in
    on that far-off shore,
they told her——*No.* Plant seedlings of *sajne* in the courtyard,
spinach vine, bottle gourd, here and there in various pots two kinds
of cactus, yellow roses;
this courtyard with its smooth floor, this portion is your life.

Thereafter

My sister used to sing wonderful Tagore songs.
She used to love reading Simone de Beauvoir.
Forgetting her midday bath, she immersed herself in Karl Marx,
      Gorky, Tolstoy, and Manik's novels.

When she wanted to feel nostalgic, Laura Ingalls Wilder was her favorite.
When she saw a play about war, I remember her crying half the night.

My sister used to read wonderful poetry;
her favorites were Shankha, Niren, Neruda, and Yevtushenko.
My sister loved the forest, not the garden;
she liked sculpture so much she once bought a ticket for Paris.

Now in my sister's poetry notebook
she keeps meticulous accounts of green vegetables,
now she walks around very proudly, loaded with metal ornaments.
She says with pride she no longer thinks about politics.
Let culture go to hell, she couldn't care less.
Dust collects on her *sitar,* mice nest in her *tanpura.*
Now she's a smart shopper, bringing home

porcelain dinnerware, fresh carp, and expensive-looking bed sheets.

The Wheel

They've dressed her in red
because red is a flashy color, it catches the eye.
They've put a necklace at her throat, the necklace that
around the neck of a helpless animal is made of rope
        and for feasts and festivals is of paper.

Her ears have been pierced, along with her nose.
Those ears and that nose are wearing metal things;
because she's got so little lustre of her own
        the lustre of metal or gems
brightens her up.

They've put bangles on her wrists
their shapes much like handcuffs, like shackles.
There are jingly bracelets on her ankles
so that her whereabouts are known to all.
There is paint applied to her face
like color upon some lifeless thing.
As if her eyes, her cheeks, her lips were not exact
as if without some added coating she weren't enough,
                                she weren't complete.

A person is turned into merchandise like this,
she's merchandise in the villages, merchandise in town,
she's on the sidewalks, the streets,
she's in the slums, the aristocratic locales,
she's in this country, and all over the place abroad.
In various ways, at various rates she's merchandise.

She is sold,
sold openly.
In some places these sales have been quite modernized.
Some applaud this modernization in the name of women's progress.

Most stupid women willingly tangle themselves in chains
            to fulfill some desire.
Those who break their chains think that they have emerged;
in fact they too get entangled some way or other
                              in another chain.

Unbearable Life Together

You have ruined my life.

At my sturdy form you hurled such a grenade of invading germs
that as long as I live, I'll suffer,
reeling from a diseased womb, diseased lungs and liver.
The one who swam backstroke all day long, played jump rope,
    her favorite, keep-away,
who was crazy about travel,
how is it she lies here flat in bed, oranges
and grapes piled on her night table?
Why did you hurl torn-up shoes
arrows of ridicule at my unblemished joy?
You've dragged all my beauty down into the gutter,
there's not even one speck left of me.
Who else could bring such utter ruin on another?

You could.
Because it's you, I accept this whole unbearable life.

II

FROM

Nirbasita bahire antare
(Banished Without and Within)

1989 and 1990

Acquaintance

As much as I had thought him to be a male,
that much he is not.
Half-neutered he is,
half a male.

A life goes by,
and you may sit and lie with a man, but
     how much can you come to know the real man?
He whom I so long thought
I knew correctly—
he whom I know is nothing like that;
in fact, he's the one I most don't know.

As much as I had thought him to be a man,
that much he is not;
half beast he is,
half a man.

Happy Marriage

My life,
like a sandbar, has been taken over by a monster of a man.
He wants my body under his control
so that if he wishes he can spit in my face,
    slap me on the cheek
and pinch my rear.
So that if he wishes he can rob me of my clothes
and take the naked beauty in his grip.
So that if he wishes he can pull out my eyes,
so that if he wishes he can chain my feet,
if he wishes, he can, with no qualms whatsoever,
    use a whip on me,
if he wishes he can chop off my hands, my fingers.
If he wishes he can sprinkle salt in the open wound,
he can throw ground-up black pepper in my eyes.
So that if he wishes he can slash my thigh with a dagger,
so that if he wishes he can string me up and hang me.

He wanted my heart under his control
so that I would love him:
in my lonely house at night,
sleepless, full of anxiety,
clutching at the window grille,
    I would wait for him and sob.
My tears rolling down, I would bake homemade bread;
so that I would drink, as if they were ambrosia,
the filthy liquids of his polygynous body.
So that, loving him, I would melt like wax,
not turning my eyes toward any other man,
I would give proof of my chastity all my life.
So that, loving him
on some moonlit night I would commit suicide
    in a fit of ecstasy.

Border

I'm going to move ahead.
Behind me my whole family is calling,
my child is pulling at my *sari*-end,
my husband stands blocking the door,
but I will go.
There's nothing ahead but a river
I will cross.
I know how to swim, but they
won't let me swim, won't let me cross.

There's nothing on the other side of the river
      but a vast expanse of fields,
but I'll touch this emptiness once
and run against the wind, whose whooshing sound
makes me want to dance. I'll dance someday
and then return.

I've not played keep-away for years
      as I did in childhood.
I'll raise a great commotion playing keep-away someday
and then return.

For years I haven't cried with my head
      in the lap of solitude.
I'll cry to my heart's content someday
and then return.

There's nothing ahead but a river
and I know how to swim.
Why shouldn't I go? I'll go.

With a Bad Dream Yesterday

Late yesterday evening in the Bangla Academy field
I met a bad dream.
The bad dream was eating peanuts, joking with his pals.
Toying with a couple of peanut shells,
I gazed into the bad dream's eyes.
In the bad dream's eyes was the hazy color of twilight.

Marijuana smoke was twisting into rings in the wind,
entwining with my scarf,
and in my dreamy eyes then, the smoky sky
and on the forehead of the sky
  a hundred thousand dots of sandalpaste.
Suddenly the bad dream, not giving a damn about anyone,
grabbed me and pulled me into his arms
and devoured me with thirty-nine kisses,
  counting all the while.

The bad dream's hair was blowing in a fantastic wind,
the buttons of his shirt were open.
Drenched in the light of the moon
  I stumbled home after midnight
and the bad dream tagged along with me,
talking all the way about love.

The bad dream is totally shameless.
The night passed, and then the day,
but he never once said he would leave.

Self-Portrait

I don't believe in God,
I look upon Nature with wondering eyes.
However much I move forward grasping the hand of progress
    society's hindrances take hold of my sleeve
        and gradually pull me backwards.
I wish I could walk all through the city
    in the middle of the night,
sitting down anywhere alone to cry.

I don't believe in God.
From house to house the religion mongers
    secretly divide us into castes,
segregate the women from the human race.
I too am divided,
I too am defrauded of my human rights.
The crafty politician
gets loud applause when he rails about class exploitation,
but he cleverly suppresses all the terminology
    of women's exploitation.
All those people of supposed good character, I know them.

Throughout the world, religion has extended its eighteen talons.
In my lone brandishing, how many of its bones can I shatter,
how much can I rip discrimination's far-spreading net?

The Fault of Loneliness

Renouncing everything, I am banished without and within.
My forgotten fingernails grow long, my fingers are ailing,
my hair's a mess with neglect, my arms every which way.
Far away in this isolated place, I am alone, in exile.
In my single room even the wind is afraid to knock,
a few dogs used to howl in the middle of the night,
     or abruptly at noon,
one day even they got up and left the compound.

You are a cheat, a hypocrite from head to toe,
I know all about your lechery,
but even so it's the fault of loneliness that I go to you.
Again and again I am defiled,
immersing in dirty water, I smear my flawless body with disgrace.
Everyone knows about your lechery,
but even so it's the fault of loneliness I go
     knocking again at your door.

People mistakenly think this is love.

Pleasure with a Woman

On the third day after we met
you objected to the way I addressed you.
By the seventh day you wanted to take me
to Madras, Bangalore, Kathmandu and back to Calcutta.
On the eighteenth day you wanted the touch of my fingers.
By the second month you demanded a kiss,
after three and a half months, my body.

What you can get from this shapely body of mine
you can get from an ordinary wife at home, or from a few
        women subordinates at the office
and even from streetwalkers available at cheap rates.
But still you're wearing out the soles of your shoes
        circling around me,
with various ruses trying to pull me near,
distracting me as you make your closing moves.
There's just one way to interpret this.
Without the thrill of seduction in enjoying a woman
you get no satisfaction from enjoying her, no
        fragrant belch of satisfaction.

And since I know this,
before anyone spits on this body of mine,
I'll spit at least twice on your filthy mind.

Divorce Letter

If you go any distance, you'll no more be mine;
you'll become everybody's playboy.

Going to any body,
picking like a vulture at the form and flesh,
    you make your meal.
You perceive no difference between the whore's
    and the lover's body.

You prefer cunning to poetry.
As night descends, one hundred and one unbridled horses
gallop stampeding through your blood,
the ancestors wake up dancing the rhumba in your blood.
I've told you a lot about moonlight;
you perceive no difference between
    the new moon and the full.
You prefer affluence to love.
From beneath anybody's heel you lick up
a drop of liquor, you're immersed from head to foot
    in thousands of gallons of liquor,
                but still your thirst isn't slaked.
I've told you a lot about dreams;
you perceive no difference between the sea and the sewer.
If you go any distance, you'll become everybody's playboy.

He who is everybody's man is never mine.

Dark and Handsome

When I see you
I want to start my life all over again.
When I see you
I want to die, and dying, turn to holy water.
If you're thirsty sometime, you may touch that water.

I'll give you my sky,
sunlight, rain, whatever you please, just take it.
Embracing your sleeplessness, I'll give you my morphine.

Give me a night twelve years long
in which to see you.
You're more moon than the moon,
in your moonlight I arrange my hair.
Putting vermilion on my forehead someday,
     I'll dress myself up as a woman waiting for her lover.

When I see you
I want to die. If you put fire
in my mouth, I'll die and go to heaven.

Body Theory

This body of mine, known so long,
at times even I can't recognize it.
If a rough hand
with various tricks touches my sandalpaste-smeared hand,
in the house of my nerves a bell chimes,
        a bell chimes.

This my own body,
this body's language I can't read;
it tells its story itself in its own language.
Then fingers, eyes, these lips, these smooth feet,
none of them are mine.
This hand is mine only
yet I don't correctly recognize this hand;
these lips are mine only, these are my breasts, buttocks, thighs;
none of these muscles, none of these pores,
are under my command, under my control.

In the two-story house of my nerves
        a bell chimes.
In this world whose plaything am I, then,
man's or Nature's?

In fact, not man
but Nature plays me,
I am the *sitar* of its whims.

At man's touch, I
wake up, breaking out of my slumbering childhood;
in my sea, a sudden high tide begins.
If the sweet scent of love is found in my blood and flesh,
it's Nature only that plays me,
I am the *sitar* of its whims.

At the Back of Progress . . .

The fellow who sits in the air-conditioned office
is the one who in his youth raped
                    a dozen or so young girls,
and at the cocktail party, he's secretly stricken with lust
fastening his eyes on the bellybutton of some lovely.
In the five-star hotels, this fellow frequently
        tries out his different tastes
        in sex acts with a variety of women.
This fellow goes home and beats his wife
                    over a handkerchief
                    or a shirt collar.
This fellow sits in his office and talks with people
                        while puffing on a cigarette
                        and shuffling through his files.
        Ringing the bell he calls his employee,
                                    shouts at him,
            orders the bearer to bring tea
                                    and drinks.
    This fellow gives out character references for people.

The employee speaks in such a low voice
that no one knows or would ever suspect
how much he could raise his voice at home,
        how foul his language could be,
        how vile his behavior.
Gathering with his buddies, he buys some movie tickets
and, kicking back on the porch outside, indulges
        in loud harangues on politics, art, and literature.

Someone is committing suicide   his mother
                                       or his grandmother
                                       or his great-grandmother.

Returning home he beats his wife
          over a bar of soap or
          the baby's pneumonia.

The bearer who brings the tea,
who keeps the lighter in his pocket
and who gets a couple of *taka* as a tip:
he's divorced his first wife for her sterility,
his second wife for giving birth to a daughter,
he's divorced his third wife for not bringing dowry.
Returning home, this fellow beats his fourth wife
over a couple of green chilis or a handful of cooked rice.

III

FROM

Atale antarin
(Captive in the Abyss)

1991

The Game in Reverse

The other day in Ramna Park I saw a boy buying a girl.
I'd really like to buy a boy for five or ten *taka*,
a clean-shaven boy, with a fresh shirt, combed and parted hair,
a boy on the park bench, or standing on the main road
      in a curvaceous pose—

I'd like to grab the boy by his collar
      and pull him up into a rickshaw—
tickling his neck and belly, I'd make him giggle;
bringing him home, I'd give him a sound thrashing
with high-heeled shoes, and then throw him out—
      "Get lost, bastard!"

Sticking Band-Aids on their foreheads, the boys
would doze on the sidewalks at dawn,
scratching at their scabies. Mangy dogs would lick at the yellow pus
         oozing out of the ulcers in their groins.
Seeing them, the girls would laugh with the tinkling sound
      of glass bangles breaking.

I really want to buy me a boy,
a fresh, nubile boy with a hairy chest—
I'll buy a boy and rough him up all over.
Kicking him hard in his shriveled balls,
      I'll shout— "Get lost, bastard!"

Aggression

Human nature is such
that if you sit, they'll say—"No, don't sit."
If you stand, "What's the matter, walk!"
And if you walk, "Shame on you, sit down!"

If you so much as lie down, they'll bother you—"Get up."
If you don't lie down, no respite, "Lie down for a bit!"

I'm wasting my days getting up and sitting down.
If I'm dying right now, they speak up—"Live."
If they see me living, who knows when
     they'll say—"Shame on you, die!"

In tremendous fear I secretly go on living.

Something or Other

There are some gluttonous men
who think that women are fresh cuts of veal,
who think they're mango jelly, boiled eggs or
      sweets made of milk.

Some sick men
think of women as diseases, stagnant pools,
      garbage dumps full of parasites;
they think of them as the inferior sex,
      the forlorn creatures of the earth.

Some religious fanatic cowards
think of women as grotesque life-forms
fashioned from men's leftover ribs,
tasty morsels offered up for amorous sport.

There'll always be some shit in this world,
some fetid essence.

Another Life

Women spend the afternoon squatting on the porch,
        picking lice from each other's hair;
they spend the evening feeding the little ones
        and lulling them to sleep in the glow of the bottle lamp.
The rest of the night they offer their backs
        to be slapped and kicked by the men of the house
or sprawl half-naked on the hard wooden cot—

Crows and women greet the dawn together.
Women blow into the oven to start the fire,
tap on the back of the winnowing tray with five fingers
        and with two fingers pick out stones.

Women spend half their lives picking stones from the rice.

Stones pile up in their hearts,
there's no one to touch them with two fingers . . .

Fire

He is my husband, the dictionary says that he's my
chief, lord, master, et cetera et cetera.
Society agrees that he's my only god.

My doddering old husband has learned well
the prevailing rules and regulations to exert authority.
He's very eager to stroll over the bridge of eternity
        to the glittering realm of paradise,
he wants all kinds of fruits, brightly colored cordials and delicious foods,
he lusts after
the fair-skinned bodies of *houris* to chew, suck and lick.

Nothing's written on my forehead but ill fate,
I spend my lifespan in society thrusting chunks of firewood
        into the oven of these earthly days.
In the afterlife I see my doddering husband
        exult over the seventy-seven pleasures of sex.

I am alone, in the joyous gardens of paradise I'm alone.
Watching the blind obscenity of men
I burn inside in the everlasting fires of hell,
        a chaste and virtuous woman.

Female Goods

Woman, you'd like a woman?
All kinds of women,
fair-skinned women, tall women, hair down to their knees,
slim waist, firm and shapely figure.
She's got no fat, no salt, you won't find
    any wrinkles in her skin.

Pierced nose, pierced ears, pierced digestive tract,
check with your fingers that nothing else is pierced.
No hand has touched her virgin limbs, her liquids
    have not spilled, a woman not yet enjoyed.
Woman, you'd like a woman?

Feed her three square meals a day,
give her *saris,* ornaments, and good soap
    to smooth on her body.
She won't raise her eyes, she won't raise her voice,
    she's a shy and modest woman,
she can cook seven dishes for one midday meal.

This female item can be used any way you like!
If you wish, chain her feet, chain her hands,
    put her mind in chains.
If you wish, divorce her, say divorce,
    and you've divorced her.

A Few Words

"They're selling one thing in every house."
—Who are *they?*
"Women."
—What are they selling?
"Freedom."
—What do the buyers give in exchange?
"Some give food, some a couple of *saris* to wear,
    and some the routine weekly sex act."
—In this world there's nothing greater than freedom.
    Freedom's never up for sale. In the eyes of human law
    this must be illegal trafficking.
"This is such a burden on society."
—How so?
"This society doesn't recognize her freedom as legal, if she is a woman."
—What if she's able to stand up with a straight spine
    and walk on her own?
"Not even then."
—If she relies on herself for food and clothing to survive,
    if she's able to speak, to laugh?
"Not even then.
    It is our social custom to jeer at those
    who can't be sold in this market."
—Who made up this custom?
"Some men."
—Oh great, fine. Men know very well
    the tricks and sundry rules of the trade.

Dirt on Women's Faces

You're smearing your cheeks, painting your eyes, putting lipstick on your lips.
Those who taught you to apply colors, put this paintbrush in your hand,
those who introduced you to the gutter's course, sunk you in muddy water,
look how they're standing there amused at the sight of you.
They're winking, licking their lips, clapping their hands.

They explained how to climb a tree as they cut the tree at its base
and you, stupid foolish girl, rush to get up it;
striking at your own feet with an ax, you break off at the root.
In fact, with your own hand you're smearing whitewash on your cheeks,
with your own hand smearing soot around your eyes.

Eve Oh Eve

Why won't Eve eat of the fruit?
Didn't Eve have a hand to reach out with,
fingers with which to make a fist;
didn't Eve have a stomach to feel hunger with,
a tongue to feel thirst,
a heart with which to love?

But then why won't Eve eat of the fruit?

Why would Eve merely suppress her wishes,
regulate her steps?
Subdue her thirst?
Why would Eve be so compelled
to keep Adam moving around in the Garden of Eden
        all their lives?

Because Eve has eaten of the fruit
        there are sky and earth,
because she has eaten
        there are moon, sun, rivers and seas.
Because she has eaten, trees, plants and vines,
because Eve has eaten of the fruit
        there is joy, because she has eaten there is joy,
joy, joy—
Eating of the fruit, Eve made a heaven of the earth.

Eve, if you get hold of the fruit
        don't ever refrain from eating.

Things Cheaply Had

In the market nothing can be had as cheaply as women.
If they get a small bottle of *alta* for their feet
    they spend three nights sleepless for sheer joy.
If they get a few bars of soap to scrub their skin
    and some scented oil for their hair
they become so submissive that they scoop out
    chunks of their flesh
to be sold in the flea market twice a week.
If they get a jewel for their nose
    they lick feet for seventy days or so,
a full three and a half months
    if it's a single striped *sari*.

Even the mangy cur of the house barks now and then,
but over the mouths of women cheaply had,
    there's a lock,
a golden lock.

IV

FROM

Behula eka bhasiyechila bhela
(Behula Floated the Raft Alone)

1993;

AND

Ay kasta jhepe, jiban debo mepe
(Pain Come Pouring Down, I'll Measure Out
My Life For You)

1994

Story

One of those boys who look as if they need to be spoonfed
said to me one day—"I'm in such pain."
Putting my heavy finger in his thick hair I said—
"The fields are flooded with white moonlight,
    let's go get drenched.
Let's cross the forest at cloudy dawn. Let's swim against
    the Sitalaksha River's current."

The boy said—"I'm really famished these days."
I gave him *ilish*-fish in mustard sauce, *chital*-fish chops,
shrimp in curried coconut, and a whole roast chicken to eat.
After the meal, a *paan* in silver foil.

The food was eaten. The drenching took place in the moonlit night.
The forest of dawn was crossed, the boy's spirits perked up too.
Around midday, his stomach and his spirits full
    the boy said—"I'm off."

One day I suddenly see him telling the girl next door
about his hunger and pain;
the girl is sitting him down, feeding him.

Straight Path

If you wish to fall in love, fall.
Look, I've stretched out my smooth arms,
if you wish, catch hold.

I don't have time to go on standing on the path.
If you have to draw back your hands,
if we don't agree,
get out of my way.

Shame, 7 December 1992

The plan was that Satipada Das would come to my house that morning
and have tea and snacks. He would play chess and gossip
     to his heart's content.
Satipada comes every day, but not today, the news came that
a gang of men with *tupis* on their heads stormed into Satipada's house,
poured gasoline over everything in the rooms, the tables and chairs,
the beds, wardrobes, pots and pans,
clothing, books.
Then they quickly lit a whole lot of matchsticks and tossed them
     in all the gasoline-soaked places.
As the fires flared up, Satipada stood stunned in the courtyard and watched
the black smoke spreading over their Tatibazar, over
     Tatibazar's patch of indifferent sky.

In the evening I went to Satipada's house and saw
Satipada sitting alone upon the ash and charred wood
of his forefathers' ancestral home, blood running down
his body, dark bruises on his chest and back.

Out of shame I could not touch him.

Mosque, Temple

Let the pavilions of religion be ground to bits,
let the bricks of temples, mosques, *gurudwaras,* churches
    be burned in blind fire,
and upon those heaps of destruction
let lovely flower gardens grow, spreading their fragrance,
let children's schools and study halls grow.

For the welfare of humanity, now let prayer halls
be turned into hospitals, orphanages, schools, universities,
now let prayer halls become academies of art, fine arts centers,
    scientific research institutes,
now let prayer halls be turned to golden rice fields
    in the radiant dawn,
open fields, rivers, restless seas.

From now on let religion's other name be humanity.

Bad Omen

Kalyani was carried off by one or more, her
torn *sari* lies there in the room,
bed and pillow all messed up,
shattered glass bangles,
drops of blood on the floor, tracks from some shoes, cigarette butts.
Perhaps after this Kalyani will be
lying in the jungle, in darkness, alone, her swollen, naked body
will be sniffed by packs of jungle dogs, flocks
of vultures will descend to peck and devour chunks of her flesh.
Seeing Kalyani, people will press handkerchiefs to their mouths
        and say, "Aha."
They'll say the girl was such a sweet-natured girl,
        even when they slapped her around
she didn't say a word, she was so awfully shy.

And if she comes and stands at the door
of her house, with her wounded, bloody, chewed up,
torn and mangled body, will her
grief-distracted mother lovingly touch
        and nurse back to health her daughter's
man-defiled form?
Or will her relatives, close neighbors, friends, anyone?

Or maybe derision will play in the pupils of their eyes,
some will cover their mouths and laugh, some will say
the girl brought bad luck, she was totally shameless too.
The *sari*-cloth over her breast used to slip off all the time,
she reddened her lips with *paan,* or she used to laugh
and roll around laughing so much that she paid no heed to men.
And this doesn't happen to anyone else,

why is she the only one in such a mess,
the girl was most certainly bad.

Kalyani's bad for sure now
and those who carried her off,
those worthy sons, they
are the wealth of this crippled nation.

Granary

You are my love's granary,
I pour out my water-steeped fertility
unstintingly, to stop does not occur to me.

Suddenly I see you've slipped away;
I search for you, my heart-usurping boy, then
find you've fled, there was a ladder in back to step down.

Flute

The cowherds don't play flutes anymore these days,
they smoke hookahs and cough,
their lungs full of sores.
Thin cows and buffaloes with water-laden eyes,
eyes full of pity, desolate fields, gaze at the indifferent sky.

The afternoon rolls on, the trees' magical shadows gradually lengthen,
the cowherds suffer from breathing pain,
sit panting in the blazing sun, stare
at the grassless, dusty fields.
The sound of sighs comes drifting, the sound
drifts of wailing winds, of wild beasts' paws, of death—

So many sounds—
only the sound of the flute is absent from this sound-filled land of terror.

Noorjahan

They have made Noorjahan stand in a hole in the courtyard,
there she stands, submerged to her waist with head hanging.
They're throwing stones at Noorjahan,
those stones are striking my body.

Stones are striking my head, forehead, chest and back,
they're throwing stones and laughing aloud, laughing and shouting abuse.
Noorjahan's fractured forehead pours out blood, mine also.
Noorjahan's eyes have burst, mine also.
Noorjahan's nose has been smashed, mine also.
Through Noorjahan's torn breast, her heart has been pierced, mine also.
Are these stones not striking you?

They're laughing aloud, laughing and stroking their beards,
there are *tupis* stuck to their heads, they too are shaking with laughter.
They're laughing and swinging their walking sticks;
from the quiver of their cruel eyes, arrows speed to pierce her body,
     my body also.
Are these arrows not piercing your body?

Poverty

What is our poverty made of?
Some say of rice, of fish,
some sigh and say of clothing,
some few think for two or ten minutes, shake their heads up and down,
it seems the lack of housing is too much.

But nobody has said anything
about another simple sort of poverty,
that is of thought.
If we eat and dress is this lack done away with?
The pigs that eat slime, eat nothing but slime
     and they'll spend their lives eating slime—
they've made no other commitment to life.
Will people merely grunt and eat? Dress? Sleep? That's all?
Have they no other commitment to people?

Poverty of mind must first be done away with.
If not, human life is worth no more than that of cows or donkeys.

Lady Ayesha

The caravan is moving, you're falling behind,
you must have pulled back hard on the camel's reins!
The youthful camel driver loved you very much,
your body too was secretly drenched—
you glided down from the camel's *howdah,*
in the heated sand you rolled around in love.

Word got around that you relieved yourself.
All sins excused for nature's needs.
You enjoyed the body's pleasures,
I take these too as bodily needs.

Let your strength give life to women.

Cannonade

Special Branch guards are on twenty-four hour duty in front of my door.
Who comes and who goes, when I leave, when I enter the house,
    they write down everything in a notebook,
who my friends are, whose waist I embrace as I laugh,
    whom I whisper to . . . everything.
But the things they cannot note down are
which thoughts come and go in my head,
what it is that I nurture in my consciousness.

The government has cannons and rifles
and a little mosquito like me has a sting.

Notes

Simple Talk

The head of the fish, free of bones, is regarded as a culinary delicacy among Bengalis. It is usually reserved for the most important family member, that is, the bread winner—almost always a male.

Alta is a red liquid with which South Asian women decorate the borders of their feet on ceremonial occasions, such as weddings or dance performances.

Boundary

Sajne is a kind of vegetable.

In traditional village houses, the central courtyard is made of packed earth; women sweep this floor every morning and apply a coat of fresh mud by hand to clean and smooth the surface.

Thereafter

Rabindranath Thakur (1861–1941), known as Tagore to the West, won the Nobel Prize for Literature in 1913. Manik Bandyopadhyay (1908–1956) was one of West Bengal's leading twentieth-century novelists. Shankha Ghosh (1932–) and Nirendranath Chakrabarti (1924–) are two of West Bengal's leading contemporary poets. Bengalis customarily refer to literary figures, indeed all public figures, by their first names, as a sign of respectful affection.

Porcelain and glass dishes are prized in Bengal, brought out only for special occasions.

The Wheel

Red is the most auspicious color for a young Bengali woman—the color of the vermilion worn by all married Bengali Hindu women in the part of their hair, the wedding *sari* and other garments for both Hindu and Muslim women.

Brightly colored paper necklaces are often worn by celebrants during Bengali religious and commemorative festivals; such necklaces are also draped around the necks of goats, sheep, or cattle to be sacrificed at Hindu temples or during *Id-al-Azha*, the Muslim festival of sacrifice.

Unbearable Life Together

Keep-away, the children's game in the fifth line, is called *gollachut* in Bengali. It is one of the few games for girls that permits running, shouting, and cooperating on a team—activities usually reserved for boys.

Happy Marriage

In the estuaries of the great rivers emptying into the Bay of Bengal, new shoals and sandbars are continually being formed from the tons of silt washed downstream every year. In heavily populated Bangladesh, these formations are zealously watched: as soon as they rise even slightly above the normal tideline, they are settled and cultivated. The first to take possession becomes the legal owner.

Border

On "keep-away," see note for "Unbearable Life Together" above.

With a Bad Dream Yesterday

The Bangla Academy, located in central Dhaka near Dhaka University, is the foremost institute in Bangladesh for the study of Bengali literature, language, and folklore. It is also a favorite rendezvous spot for young people, especially college and university students, who otherwise have rather limited opportunities to meet members of the opposite sex.

Sandalpaste, or sandalwood paste is a fragrant preparation applied by priests to the foreheads of worshippers at Hindu temples. Beyond its function in this religious context, it is used by both Hindus and Muslims as a perfume and skin balm.

Dark and Handsome

Bengali Hindu women put vermilion paste in the part of their hair as a sign of marriage.

In the Hindu cremation ceremony, the funeral pyre is customarily lit by the closest male relative. If a wife dies and there is no son, the husband may perform the rite. The fire is applied first to the mouth of the deceased.

Body Theory

The Bengali for "body theory" is *dehatattwa,* a Sanskrit-derived term which can also mean "anatomy" or "physiology," although most physicians simply use the English medical terms. The more immediate associations of *dehatattwa* for a Bengali reader would be the Tantric doctrine that the body is the seat of all knowledge, and its esoteric implication that sexual acts can thus be employed as spiritual exercises in the search for union with the Divine.

The Game in Reverse

Ramna Park is a large, open park in central Dhaka, next to the Dhaka University campus. It is a well-known strolling ground for prostitutes.

The *taka* is the monetary unit of Bangladesh, thirty-six to the dollar at exchange rates current in mid-1991, when this translation was completed. Five or ten *taka* would seem to be a hyperbolically low figure, but some female prostitutes—poor village girls or urban slum-dwelling women—may be had for such small sums.

The Bengali word translated here as "curvaceous" is *tribhanga* (literally, "thrice-bent"), an epithet in Hindu lore for the youthful god Krishna when he stands playing the flute, his body bent in a teasing and provocative pose.

Fire

The *houris* are the seventy-seven celestial virgins promised to all faithful male Muslims as consorts in paradise.

Female Goods

According to Islamic law, a man may divorce his wife by simply uttering the word *talak* (meaning "I divorce you") three times.

Dirt on Women's Faces

"Mukhe cunkali makha" is a derogatory expression in Bengali, meaning to smear the face with whitewash *(cun)* and soot *(kali),* that is, to disgrace oneself. The poet

divides the word *cunkali* into its two literal components to make the analogy between eyeliner (soot) and makeup or powder (whitewash).

Things Cheaply Had

For "*alta*," see the note to "Simple Talk" above.

Story

The dishes listed here are delicacies in East Bengali cuisine. *Paan* consists of betel nuts, catechu, various spices, lime, and on occasion tobacco, all of which is wrapped in betel leaves and chewed as a mild stimulant, often after meals. A *paan* wrapped in silver foil would be a special presentation for an honored guest.

Shame, 7 December 1992

The date in the poem's title refers to the riots that broke out in Bangladesh the day after the destruction of a sixteenth-century mosque in India.

To a Bengali, Satipada Das is a recognizably Hindu name for a man.

The *tupi* is the white skull cap all Muslim men wear for entering the mosque and for all solemn occasions.

Tatibazar (meaning "Weavers' Market") is a Hindu neighborhood in the old part of the city of Dhaka, the capital of Bangladesh. This neighborhood was extensively damaged in the December 1992 riots.

Mosque, Temple

Gurudwaras are the houses of worship for Sikhs.

Bad Omen

There is a play here between the original Bengali title and the name of the protagonist, Kalyani. In Bengali the title is "*Akalyan*," meaning "spiritual or moral harm, a bad omen, woe"; Kalyani, a common name usually given to Hindu girls, means "happy, beneficial, giving good health or prosperity."

Most poor women in Bengal cannot afford the ready-made blouses that are worn beneath *saris*. If the upper length of a village woman's *sari* slips off her shoulders, her breasts are exposed. To preserve modesty, these women must thus continually adjust and tighten the wrap of their *saris*.

Noorjahan

Noorjahan was a poor daughter of a landless peasant in the district of Sylhet, in northeastern Bangladesh. Divorced by her first husband, in January 1993 Noorjahan married again—a common and accepted practice among Muslims worldwide. The local *mullahs* (Muslim religious leaders), however, declared Noorjahan's second marriage to be against Islamic law. Several days later, Noorjahan was taken out to a field at dawn, buried up to her waist in a pit, and publicly stoned for alleged adultery by the *mullahs'* followers. The insult and humiliation led Noorjahan to commit suicide by ingesting insecticide.

Lady Ayesha

This poem reinterprets one of the stories found in the *Hadith,* a supplement to the Koran. While on an expedition with her husband, the Prophet Mohammad, Ayesha became separated from his caravan when she stopped to relieve herself. After a young soldier discovered her and then returned her to Mohammad's party, she was wrongly accused of adultery. One month later, a revelation exposed her innocence to Mohammad, and she was forgiven.

Cannonade

This poem refers to the period between September 1993 and April 1994 when Nasrin, following death threats from Islamic fundamentalists, lived in her Dhaka apartment, guarded by police.

Notes on the original Bengali book titles

Behula eka bhasiyechila bhela (*Behula Floated the Raft Alone*)

In Hindu lore, Behula was the wife of Lokindara, the eldest son of a wealthy merchant, Chanda. Chanda refused to worship Manasa, the snake-goddess; offended, Manasa cursed all Chanda's sons to die of snake-bite. Consequently, Lokindara was bitten by a cobra on the night of his wedding to Behula, and he died. Unable to revive him, Behula set sail in a small boat or raft (a *bhela*), and crossed the waters of the sacred River Gangura. She made her way to the abode of the gods to beg for her husband's life, which the gods restored because they were impressed with Behula's courage and fidelity—the virtues of an ideal Hindu wife. Behula's courage is proverbial for Hindu women, but Bengali Muslim women also refer to her as an example of women's enterprise and daring. Her story seems to have particular resonance for twentieth-century Bangladeshi Muslim women poets, several of whom—including Taslima Nasrin—allude to Behula's story in at least one of their poems.

Ay kasta jhepe, jiban debo mepe (*Pain Come Pouring Down, I'll Measure Out My Life For You*)

This title echoes a Bengali children's rhyme, "Ay bristi jhepe, dhan debo mepe" ("Rain come pouring down, I'll measure out my rice for you"). Unlike the venerable English-language rhyme, "Rain, rain, go away . . . ," this rhyme welcomes the rain, promising it a rich harvest of rice if it will be generous with its life-giving water. The allusions to water in both of these titles remind readers what a riverine and water-suffused land Bangladesh is.

About the Translators

Mohammad Nurul Huda was born in 1949 in Cox's Bazar, in the Chittagong district of Bangladesh; he received a B. A. with Honors and an M. A., both in English Literature, from Dhaka University. Since 1973, he has served as Assistant Director, Deputy Director and, as of 1994, Director of Planning and Training of the Bangla Academy, a research institute devoted to the study, promotion and publication of Bengali language, literature, and folklore. A prolific poet and literary essayist, Huda has published in Bengali some twenty-five volumes of poetry, half a dozen works of essays and criticism, and two novels; he is regarded as one of Bangladesh's leading poets. He has translated works from English to Bengali, among them the play *Agamemnon* and a selection of short stories by Flannery O'Connor.

Subharanjan Dasgupta was born in 1949. He lives in Calcutta, where he works as a journalist for the Ananda Bazar Patrika Group. His translations of modern Bengali poems have been published in India and abroad. He has also published several books in Bengali, among them *Bengali Poems on Calcutta* and *Dialectics and Dream.*

Farida Sarkar was born in 1957 in Rajshahi, Bangladesh; she completed her B. A. with Honors and M. A. in English Literature at Dhaka University and lectured at Notre Dame College and Eden Government Women's College in Dhaka. She also worked as an Assistant Commissioner and Assistant Secretary for the Information Ministry of the Bangladesh government, as a freelance journalist for Dhaka newspapers, and as an announcer for Radio Bangladesh. In 1991, she came to the United States on a Fulbright fellowship. In 1994, she began working for the Voice of America/Bangla Service in Washington, DC. She has published two volumes of poetry in Bengali, and her poems have appeared in most major Bangladeshi periodicals and newspapers.

Carolyne Wright was born in Seattle, received a B. A. in English from the Seattle University Honors Program, and completed an M. A. and Doctor of Arts in English and Creative Writing from Syracuse University. She lived in Calcutta from 1986 to

1988 on an Indo-U.S. Subcommission Fellowship, to collect and translate the work of twentieth-century Bengali women poets and writers with the assistance of Bengali collaborators, and to prepare anthologies and collections of this work for publication. From 1989 to 1991, she was in Dhaka on a Fulbright Senior Research Fellowship to complete this translation project. She met and began working with Taslima Nasrin in early 1990. Wright's translations from Bengali have appeared in many journals, including *The New Yorker, Kenyon Review, Triquarterly, American Poetry Review, The Spectator* (U. K.), and the *London Review of Books.* Four books of her own poems and a volume of essays have been published, and she has received several awards for her poetry and translations, including the Academy of American Poets Prize, a New York State CAPS Grant, the Pablo Neruda Prize, a Witter Bynner Foundation Grant in Poetry, the PEN/Jerard Fund Award, and an Award for Outstanding Translation from the American Literary Translators' Association. From 1991 to 1992, she was a Fellow of the Bunting Institute of Radcliffe College, and from 1992 to 1994, she was an Associate of the Department of Sanskrit and Indian Studies at Harvard University, where she edited two Bengali anthologies, *A Bouquet of Roses on the Burning Ground: Poetry by Bengali Women* and *Crossing the Seasonal River: Stories of Bengal by Women,* and worked on several other books, including a memoir about her experiences in Bengal. She lives in Arlington, Massachusetts.

The poems listed below were translated by Carolyne Wright with the following collaborators:

Farida Sarkar: "Believing Hands"; "Character"; "Run! Run!"; "Border"; "With a Bad Dream Yesterday."

Mohammad Nurul Huda: "Divided"; "Tongue"; "Simple Talk"; "Acquaintance"; "Happy Marriage" (with Taslima Nasrin); "Divorce Letter"; "Dark and Handsome"; "Body Theory"; "At the Back of Progress..."; "The Game in Reverse"; "Something or Other"; "Eve Oh Eve"; "Things Cheaply Had" (with Taslima Nasrin).

Subharanjan Dasgupta: "Story"; "Straight Path"; "Shame, 7 December 1992"; "Mosque, Temple"; "Bad Omen"; "Granary"; "Flute"; "Noorjahan"; "Poverty"; "Lady Ayesha"; "Cannonade."

All other poems were translated by Carolyne Wright.